Unchopping a Tree

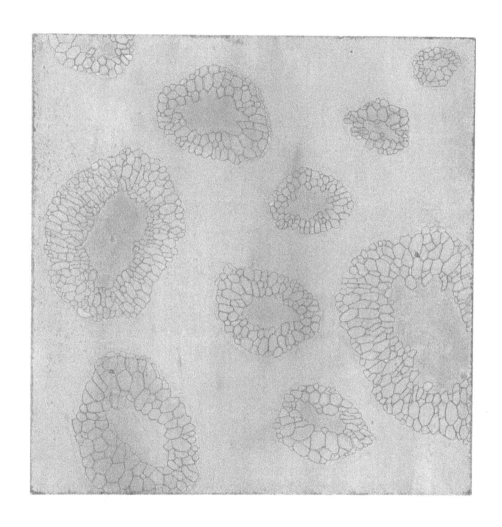

Unchopping a Tree

W. S. Merwin

Drawings by Liz Ward

The Interior Life of a Tree

trinity university press · san antonio

Tale

After many winters the moss

finds the sawdust crushed bark chips

and says old friend

old friend

Unchopping a Tree

START with the leaves, the small twigs, and the nest that have been shaken, ripped, or broken off by the fall; these must be gathered and attached once again to their respective places. It is not arduous work, unless major limbs have been smashed or mutilated.

J F THE fall was carefully and correctly planned, the chances of anything of the kind happening will have been reduced. Again, much depends upon the size, age, shape, and species of the tree. Still, you will be lucky if you can get through this stage without having to use machinery.

*E*ven in the best of circumstances

it is a labor that will make you wish often that

you had won the favor of the universe of ants,

the empire of mice, or at least a local tribe of

squirrels, and could enlist their labors and their

talents. But no, they leave you to it. They have

learned, with time. This is men's work.

IT GOES without saying that if the tree was hollow in whole or in part, and contained old nests of bird or mammal or insect, or hoards of nuts or such structures as wasps or bees build for their survival, the contents will have to be repaired where necessary, and reassembled, insofar as possible, in their original order, including the shells of nuts already opened.

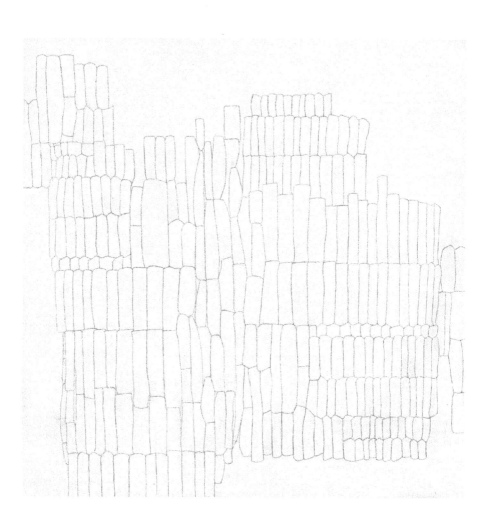

WITH spiders' webs you must simply do the best you can. We do not have the spider's weaving equipment, nor any substitute for the leaf's living bond with its point of attachment and nourishment. It is even harder to simulate the latter when the leaves have once become dry—as they are bound to do, for this is not the labor of a moment.

ALSO it hardly needs saying that this is the time for repairing any neighboring trees or bushes or other growth that may have been damaged by the fall. The same rules apply. Where neighboring trees were of the same species it is difficult not to waste time conveying a detached leaf back to the wrong tree. Practice, practice. Put your hope in that.

Now the tackle must be put into place, or the scaffolding, depending on the surroundings and the dimensions of the tree. It is ticklish work. Almost always it involves, in itself, further damage to the area, which will have to be corrected later.

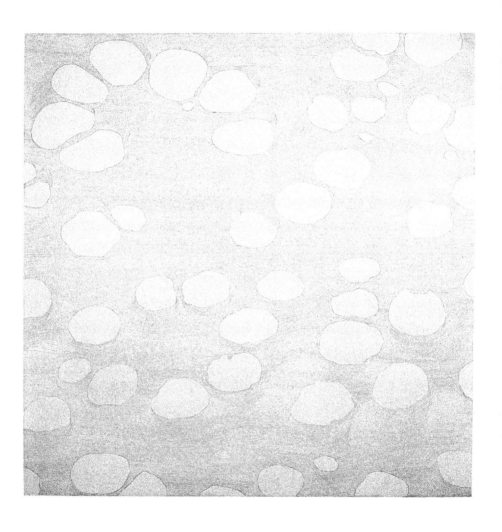

BUT as you've heard, it can't

be helped. And care now is likely to save you

considerable trouble later. Be careful to grind

nothing into the ground.

At LAST the time comes for the erecting of the trunk. By now it will scarcely be necessary to remind you of the delicacy of this huge skeleton. Every motion of the tackle, every slight upward heave of the trunk, the branches, their elaborately reassembled panoply of leaves (now dead) will draw from you an involuntary gasp.

You will watch for a leaf or a twig to be snapped off yet again. You will listen for the nuts to shift in the hollow limb and you will hear whether they are indeed falling into place or are spilling in disorder—in which case, or in the event of anything else of the kind—operations will have to cease, of course, while you correct the matter.

THE raising itself is no small

enterprise, from the moment when the chains

tighten around the old bandages until the bole

hangs vertical above the stump, splinter above

splinter.

Now the final straightening of the splinters themselves can take place (the preliminary work is best done while the wood is still green and soft, but at times when the splinters are not badly twisted most of the straightening is left until now, when the torn ends are face to face with each other).

WHEN the splinters are perfectly complementary the appropriate fixative is applied. Again we have no duplicate of the original substance. Ours is extremely strong, but it is rigid. It is limited to surfaces, and there is no play in it.

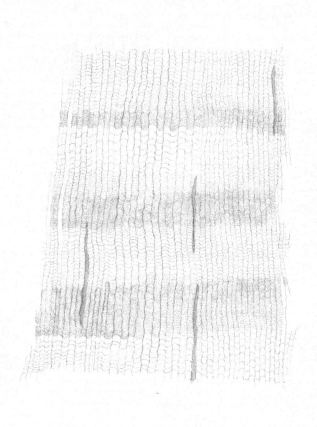

However the core is not the part of the trunk that conducted life from the roots up to the branches and back again. It was relatively inert.

THE fixative for this part is not the

same as the one for the outer layers and the bark,

and if either of these is involved in the splintered

section they must receive applications of the

appropriate adhesives. Apart from being

incorrect and probably ineffective, the

core fixative would leave a scar on the bark.

WHEN all is ready the splintered
trunk is lowered onto the splinters of the stump.
This, one might say, is only the skeleton of the
resurrection. Now the chips must be gathered,
and the sawdust, and returned to their former
positions. The fixative for the wood layers will
be applied to chips and sawdust consisting only
of wood.

*C*HIPS and sawdust consisting of several substances will receive applications of the correct adhesives. It is as well, where possible, to shelter the materials from the elements while working. Weathering makes it harder to identify the smaller fragments.

BARK sawdust in particular the earth lays claim to very quickly. You must find your own ways of coping with this problem.

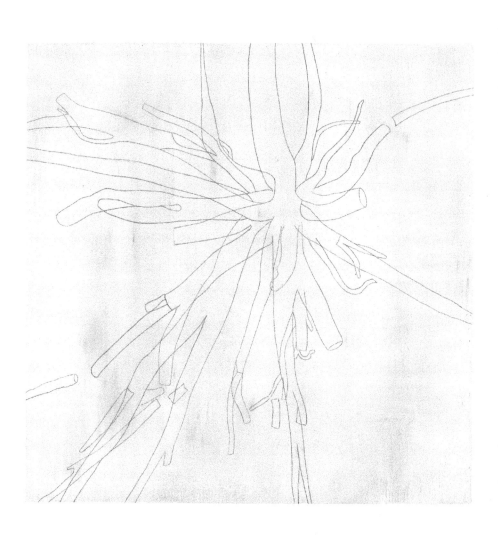

THERE is a certain beauty, you will notice at moments, in the pattern of the chips as they are fitted back into place. You will wonder to what extent it should be described as natural, to what extent man-made. It will lead you on to speculations about the parentage of beauty itself, to which you will return.

T H E adhesive for the chips is translucent, and not so rigid as that for the splinters. That for the bark and its subcutaneous layers is transparent and runs into the fibers on either side, partially dissolving them into each other.

I T DOES not set the sap flowing again but it does pay a kind of tribute to the preoccupations of the ancient thoroughfares. You could not roll an egg over the joints but some of the mineshafts would still be passable, no doubt. For the first exploring insect who raises its head in the tight echoless passages.

*T*HE day comes when it is all

restored, even to the moss (now dead) over

the wound. You will sleep badly, thinking of

the removal of the scaffolding that must begin

the next morning. How you will hope for sun

and a still day!

The removal of the scaffolding or tackle is not so dangerous, perhaps, to the surroundings, as its installation, but it presents problems. It should be taken from the spot piece by piece as it is detached, and stored at a distance.

You have come to accept it there,

around the tree. The sky begins to look naked

as the chains and struts one by one vacate their

positions.

FINALLY the moment arrives when

the last sustaining piece is removed and the tree

stands again on its own. It is as though its weight

for a moment stood on your heart.

You listen for a thud of settlement, a warning creak deep in the intricate joinery. You cannot believe it will hold. How like something dreamed it is, standing there all by itself. How long will it stand there now?

THE first breeze that touches its dead leaves all seems to flow into your mouth. You are afraid the motion of the clouds will be enough to push it over. What more can you do? What more can you do?

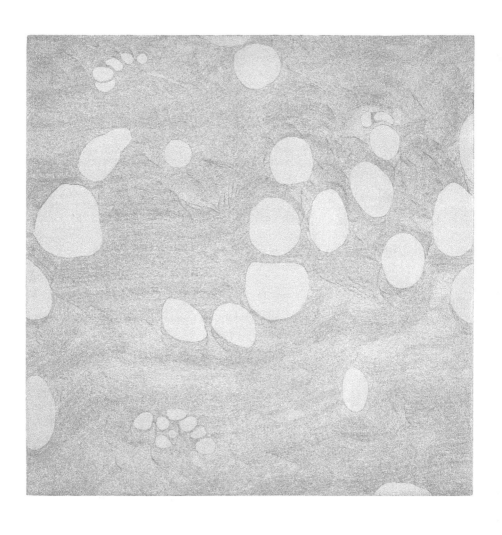

BUT there is nothing more you can do.

Others are waiting.

Everything is going to have to be put back.

W. S. MERWIN is the author of more than fifty books of poetry and prose, translation, and plays. His recent collections include *The Shadow of Sirius*, which won the 2009 Pulitzer Prize (his second) and *Migration*, which won the 2005 National Book Award. His first book of poetry, *A Mask for Janus*, won the 1952 Yale Younger Poets Prize, selected by W. H. Auden. His other honors include the Lannan Literary Award for Lifetime Achievement, the Bollingen Prize, the Ruth Lilly Poetry Prize, the Dorothea Tanning Prize, the PEN Translation Prize, the Wallace Stevens Award, and a Lila Wallace-Reader's Digest Writers' Award, as well as fellowships from the National Endowment for the Arts, the Academy of American Poets, and the Rockefeller and Guggenheim Foundations. He has served as a U.S. poet laureate. In 2013 Merwin was named the first laureate of the Zbigniew Herbert International Literary Award in Warsaw. A dedicated environmentalist, he has spent the last thirty years planting nineteen acres with over 800 species of palm, creating a sustainable forest that is now the Merwin Conservancy. He lives on the island of Maui, in Hawai'i.

LIZ WARD's paintings, drawings and prints are
informed by natural history and the environmental crisis.
Her work has been widely exhibited and is represented
in many private and public collections. Ward completed
many of the drawings in this book with the support of a
Brown Foundation fellowship for a residency at the Dora
Maar House in Ménerbes, France. She is a professor
of art at Trinity University, and she lives and works in
Castroville, Texas.

The drawings for *The Interior Life of a Tree* were
completed between 2005 and 2013. Ward used studies
of the cellular structure of trees that ranged from root
structures to the vascular system. The drawings on the
frontispiece and opposite pages 9, 15, 21, 27, 33, and 41
were done with silverpoint and tinted gesso on paper.
The drawings opposite pages 13, 19, 37, and 45 were
done with silverpoint and tinted gesso on panel.

Published by Trinity University Press
San Antonio, Texas 78212

We gratefully acknowledge the support of Martin and Heather Catto Kohout
of Madroño Ranch: A Center for Writing, Art, and the Environment in
Medina, Texas, in the publication of this book.

Design by David Bullen

ISBN 978-1-59534-307-9 paperback

CIP data on file at the Library of Congress

28 27 25 25 24   5 4 3 2 1

Printed in the USA
CPSIA information can be obtained
at www.ICGtesting.com
JSHW072213100124
55145JS00008B/10

9 781595 343079